# EXPLORE

THE
MEANING
OF

Published in North America by Alpha North America, 2275 Half Day Road Suite 185, Deerfield, IL 60015

© 2010 Alpha International, Holy Trinity Brompton, Brompton Road, London SW7 1JA, UK

*The Alpha Course Team Manual*

This edition first printed by Alpha North America in 2010

Printed in the United States of America

Scripture in this publication is from the Holy Bible, New International Version (NIV), Copyright 1973, 1978, 1984 International Bible Society, used by permission of Zondervan. All rights reserved.

ISBN 978-1-934564-28-8

3  4  5  6  7  8  9  10  Printing/Year 15  14  13  12

# CONTENTS

**SECTION 1    SMALL GROUP DISCUSSION**                                        4

Suggestions for Small Groups                                                  6

Hosts and Helpers Preparation                                                 7

**Session 1**   Who Is Jesus?                                                 9

**Session 2**   Why Did Jesus Die?                                          11

**Session 3**   How Can We Have Faith?                                      13

**Session 4**   Why and How Do I Pray?                                      15

**Session 5**   Why and How Should I Read the Bible?                        17

**Session 6**   How Does God Guide Us?                                      19

**Session 7**   Who Is the Holy Spirit?                                     21

**Session 8**   What Does the Holy Spirit Do?                               23

**Session 9**   How Can I Be Filled with the Holy Spirit?                   25

**Session 10**  How Can I Resist Evil?                                      27

**Session 11**  Why and How Should I Tell Others?                           29

**Session 12**  Does God Heal Today?                                        31

**Session 13**  What about the Church?                                      33

**Session 14**  How Can I Make the Most of the Rest of My Life?             35

**SECTION 2    TEAM TRAINING**                                             36

**Team Training 1**   Hosting Small Groups                                  38

**Team Training 2**   Pastoral Care                                         48

**Team Training 3**   Prayer Ministry on Alpha                              56

# SUGGESTIONS FOR SMALL GROUPS

The aim of this manual is to provide you with practical tips and suggestions to help you host your Alpha small group effectively. Obviously, the discussion questions will not be necessary if the conversation arises naturally. You will probably only use one per topic, and hope to let things flow from there. The questions are intended to be as open and non-threatening as possible. These are only suggestions, so do use any method or questions that you find helpful.

If you are running Alpha as a discipleship course or if your guests are already Christians, you can also use the optional Bible studies provided.

## Helpful general questions:

How did you respond to tonight's talk?

What did you feel about tonight's talk?

What did you think about tonight's talk?

Did anything that was said tonight particularly speak to you or surprise you?

What issues were raised for you by tonight's talk?

Is this a new subject for anyone?

Note: At the end of the course there is an Alpha celebration evening, giving people the opportunity to invite potential guests to hear the talk, "Is There More to Life than This?" There is no small group time after the introductory talk.

Talks 7, 8, 9 and 14 are given on the Alpha weekend.

# HOSTS AND HELPERS PREPARATION

- Each job within the team is vitally important. If you are unable to do the job you've been given, please let the director know as soon as you can

- Remember, you are the hosts! Make sure newcomers feel welcomed and looked after

- When you have finished your discussion, it would be great if you could tidy your group's area

- Please ensure that everyone goes to the admin/prayer meeting at the start – there are important notices and helpful reminders given each week. For the first couple of weeks, the meeting will be slightly extended

## RUNNING ORDER SUGGESTIONS

Here is a suggested schedule for an evening Alpha course. Adjust the actual times to fit your situation. Always allow forty-five minutes for the small group time.

**5:15 P.M.** (Weeks 1 and 2 only): Administrative and prayer meeting for leaders and helpers. Small group assignments and meeting places are clarified. Each set of leaders and helpers decides who will serve as greeters, dinner host, and runners (to cover last-minute details.)

**5:30 P.M.** (Weeks 3–10): Leaders and helpers arrive for administrative and prayer meeting. Use this time to pray for each small group member and to make sure everyone is clear on his or her responsibilities. Everyone should know the exact meeting place for dinner and small groups.

**5:45 P.M.** The administrative and prayer meeting ends. All leaders and helpers go to their assigned tasks. It is very important to welcome people as they arrive, making sure that everyone (including yourself) has a name tag each week.

**6:00 P.M.** Dinner is served. To build unity in the small groups, group members should eat together weekly. (Many people may have friends they want to talk and sit with, but they should be encouraged to remain with their small group.)

To avoid lines and allow visiting time, dinner should be served as quickly as possible. Money for dinner can be collected when it is served.

Have additional Alpha resources available for purchase.

**6:30 P.M.** The Alpha course talk (talk numbers correspond with Alpha course DVDs). Encourage groups to move seats into semicircle for announcements, worship, and talk.

It is best to hold the Weekend or Day Away after Talk 7 and before Talk 10. Talks 8–10 and 15 are usually covered during the Weekend. Always have the talk on resisting evil after the Weekend.

**7:45 P.M.** Talk ends
Book sales should be open
Coffee

**8:00 P.M.** Helpers should help people to find their small groups and to join them promptly. Don't forget those who were not there the previous week.

**8:15 P.M.** Weeks 1–8 and 10: Small groups begin.
Week 9: Talk 13 is followed by a time of prayer ministry.

**9:00 P.M.** Small groups end.

Note: It is very important to start and end each part of the evening on time.

* Running times have been given as a guide only

# WHO IS JESUS?

## SESSION 1: WHO IS JESUS?

### PRACTICAL

Welcome everyone to the group.

Pass an address form around the group for the guests to fill in. Explain that this form helps administratively, but it's not essential if a guest is uncomfortable.

Icebreakers

- Name Game
  Explain that this is a silly game—but the best way for everyone to learn each other's names at the first session

### To play the name game:
  - Each person tries to think of an adjective that would describe them. It must also have the same first letter as their name. For example, "Jovial John" or "Happy Helen"
  - Each person says what their name is and why. For example, Jovial John is jovial because he has a hearty laugh
  - Each person has a go at repeating all the names of the guests preceding them from memory

- **Desert island**
  Ask guests to respond to the following question:
  - If you were stranded on a desert island, what three things would you want to take with you?

  or, as an alternative:

  - If your house was on fire and you could only go back and get one thing, what would you get?

- **What made you decide to do an Alpha course?**
  Start with someone who is likely to admit they are an atheist/agnostic. This gives the rest of the group permission to say what they really think. (If you start with someone who turns out to be an enthusiastic Christian already, it may be harder for the others to feel comfortable about being honest about their lack of belief.)

  Write down the questions so that you can come back to them later in the course

- If you could ask God one question and guarantee an answer, what would you ask?

## DISCUSSION

1. Before you heard the talk tonight, what was your concept of Jesus? Has it changed? If so, in what way?

2. What aspects of the evidence presented tonight did you find convincing/not convincing?

3. Who do you think Jesus is?

4. If you had a chance to meet Jesus, how would you feel and what would you say to Him?

WHY DID JESUS DIE?

## SESSION 2: WHY DID JESUS DIE?

### PRACTICAL

Introduce any new guests. Pass around the address list. Add any new names and addresses and correct any mistakes from the previous week.

### DISCUSSION

This is often the week when the subject of "suffering" arises (see *Searching Issues*, booklet: *Why Does God Allow Suffering?*).

1. What is your reaction to the crucifixion?

2. Do you feel that sin is an outdated concept or is it something you can relate to?

3. How do you respond to the word "sin" and the word "forgiveness"?

4. Would you agree that sin is addictive? What do you see as the consequences of sin, if any?

## OPTIONAL BIBLE STUDY:

**Luke 15:11–24**
**The parable of the prodigal son**

**1. Why do you think that the son decided to leave home? What was he hoping for?**
- "Wild living" (v. 13)
- "Give me" (v. 11) selfishness/sin

**2. What was life like in the far country?**
- Wasting his life (v. 13)
- Began to see the need (v. 14)
- Severe famine (v. 14)
- Hunger (v. 15)
- Loneliness (v. 15)

**3. How does this compare with your experience of life?**

**4. What made him decide to go home?**
- Thinks about situation
- "He came to his senses" (v. 17)

**5. What does he decide to do?**
- Act of the will (v. 18)
- Action (v. 20)

**6. What does the picture of the father tell us about what God is like?** (vv. 20–24)

## SESSION 3: HOW CAN WE HAVE FAITH?

### PRACTICAL

Introduce any new guests. Pass around the address list and amend if needed.

This is a good week to mention the Alpha weekend for the first time. Give the dates to the guests.

### DISCUSSION

You may find that people have questions, for example, about other religions (see *Searching Issues* booklet: *What about Other Religions?*).

1. What would you write on a form where it asked your religion?

2. Do you associate love or fear with God?

3. When it is said that Christianity will make a change in your character, how do you feel?

4. What does the idea of a relationship with God suggest to you?

## OPTIONAL BIBLE STUDY:

1 Peter 1:3–8

1. What do you think Peter means by
   "new birth?" (v. 3)

2. What does the future hold for
   Christians? (v. 4)
   (compare hopes of the world)

3. How can we be so sure about the
   future?
   • Resurrection
   • Shielded by God's power (v. 5)

4. In what light should we see our
   problems?
   • Relative shortness (v. 6)
   • Their purpose (v. 7)

5. What do we learn from verse 8 about
   our relationship with Jesus Christ?
   • Our love for Him
   • The joy

# WHY AND HOW DO I...

# PRAY?

## SESSION 4: WHY AND HOW DO I PRAY?

### PRACTICAL

This is a good week to encourage people about the Alpha weekend. Mention the cost and the possibility of scholarships.

### DISCUSSION

1. Have you ever tried praying? What happened?

2. What do you think about the idea of God answering prayer?

3. Can anyone describe a time when a "coincidence" happened?

4. In the talk, various reasons for praying are given. Which of these do you relate to and why?

## OPTIONAL BIBLE STUDY

**Matthew 6:5–13**
**The Lord's Prayer**

1. Do verses 5–6 suggest that it's wrong to pray in public? What is Jesus really getting at?

• Need for sincerity

2. What can you do to reduce the distractions that get in the way of your time alone with God? (v. 6)

• Need for secrecy

3. What are the differences between pagan and Christian prayer? (v. 7)

4. What is the difference between the repetition in prayer that Jesus denounces and the persistence in prayer that He recommends? (v. 7)

• Need for simplicity

5. How could you apply the requests of the Lord's Prayer more to your own life?

• Need for more structure

6. Take time to talk about any answers to prayer that you have seen recently.

# WHY HOW I THE AND SHOULD READ BIBLE?

## SESSION 5: WHY AND HOW SHOULD I READ THE BIBLE?

### PRACTICAL

Remind the group about the Alpha weekend. Ask someone who has benefited from a previous one to describe their experience. Take further names and collect payment.

### DISCUSSION

1. Have you ever read the Bible? How did it go for you?

2. Have you ever read a modern translation of the Bible?

3. Have you read anything in the Bible that has challenged an aspect of your beliefs or behavior?

4. What do you feel about the suggestion that the Bible is a "manual for life"?

5. "What the Scriptures said, God said." Do you share that view?

## OPTIONAL BIBLE STUDY

Mark 4:1–8, 13–20
The parable of the sower

"Parable": Putting one thing alongside another by comparison or illustration

The hard-hearted (vv. 4,15)

1. What was the problem?

2. What is the difference between hearing the word and responding?

3. Can you think of a time when you read the Bible or listened to a sermon, but it made little or no impact on your life?

The faint-hearted (vv. 5–6;16–17)

1. What was the problem?

2. What sort of things do you think Jesus meant by "trouble" and "persecution" (opposition)?

3. What do you think the roots are?

• Roots cannot be seen—the things we do in secret, such as Bible reading, prayer, giving, etc.

The half-hearted (vv. 7,18)

1. What was the problem?

2. How long did it take for the problem to become apparent?

3. How do we prevent issues such as the worries of this life, the deceitfulness of wealth and the desire for other things from choking the word?

The whole-hearted (vv. 8,20)

1. What does God promise to those who persevere?

2. What do you think the crop is?

# HOW DOES GOD GUIDE US?

## SESSION 6: HOW DOES GOD GUIDE US?

### PRACTICAL

Arrange transportation for the Alpha weekend if necessary.

### DISCUSSION

1. Has anyone had any experience in the last few weeks that they think might be God guiding them?

2. How do you feel about the idea of God having a plan for you?

3. How does God speak to people today? Have you experienced this?

4. What should we do if we believe we have made a mess of our lives?

## OPTIONAL BIBLE STUDY

**Proverbs 16:1-9**

1. **What conditions does God attach to guiding us?** (vv. 3, 5, 7)

- **Confide in God**

- **No room for pride or independence**

- **Obedience**

2. **What promises of success\* does He offer?** (vv. 6b–8)

- **Avoidance of evil**

- **Peaceful life**

\* Note: not necessarily material success

3. **How does this picture compare with your own experience?**

4. **With so much confusion in the world, how do we know that God can handle it?** (vv. 1, 4, 9)

- **God is sovereign**

- **He is in control**

## SESSION 7: WHO IS
## THE HOLY SPIRIT?

There is no small group discussion
following this session.

WHAT DOES THE HOLY SPIRIT DO?

## SESSION 8: WHAT DOES THE HOLY SPIRIT DO?

### BIBLE STUDY AND DISCUSSION

#### 1 Corinthians 12:4–11

1. Has anyone heard of or had any experience of spiritual gifts?

2. What are the spiritual gifts? (vv. 8–10) Where do these gifts come from? (v. 11) [list the gifts and explain them]

- The gifts are all from God

3. How do you feel about the idea of God giving us supernatural gifts?

4. Does everybody have the same gifts? (vv. 4–6)

- Different gifts, works, and service, but same God

5. Why does God give spiritual gifts to people? (v. 7)

- For the common good

- Not for our own glory

6. Mention that there may be an opportunity in the afternoon to hear more on this subject

# HOW CAN I BE FILLED WITH THE HOLY SPIRIT?

## SESSION 9: HOW CAN I BE FILLED WITH THE HOLY SPIRIT?

### PRACTICAL

This session is followed by a time of ministry in a corporate setting. Spend time praying with any guests who would like prayer to be filled with the Holy Spirit.

Usually, before the final session, there is an opportunity to find out how the guests in your groups have found the weekend. Ask the members of the group to describe their experience of the weekend, giving them an opportunity to ask any questions and discuss.

# HOW CAN I [RESIST]

## SESSION 10: HOW CAN I RESIST EVIL?

### PRACTICAL

Start the small group time by asking guests to share their experiences of the Alpha weekend. This gives the guests the opportunity to express what God has done in their lives. It can be a great encouragement to the group. Remember to include those who did not go on the weekend in the discussion.

### DISCUSSION

1. Do you believe in the supernatural / black magic / the occult?
2. Before tonight, did you have a concept of the devil? Has it changed?
3. Why do you think bad things happen?
4. Why do you think the world is in such a mess?

## OPTIONAL BIBLE STUDY

**Ephesians
6:10–20 The armor of God**

1. What do verses 11 and 12 tell us about the nature of the struggle in which we are involved?

- **Subtlety of attack: "devil's schemes"** (v. 11)

- **Power** (v. 12)

- **Brutality** (v. 12)

2. What do you think Paul means by "the day of evil?" (v. 13) (Discuss times of strong attack)

3. What do you think the pieces of armor represent? How do we acquire them?

- **Truth:** The Bible – the Word of God

- **Righteousness:** Doing what is right / clear conscience

- **The gospel of peace:** Telling others

- **Faith:** Opposite of cynicism / scepticism / doubt, etc.

- **Helmet of salvation:** Knowing in your head that you are saved / assurance

- **Word of God:** Regular Bible reading

- **Prayer:** Regular prayer and especially for opportunities to tell others (vv. 19–20), e.g., celebration dinner!

# WHY AND HOW SHOULD I TELL OTHERS?

## SESSION 11: WHY AND HOW SHOULD I TELL OTHERS?

### PRACTICAL

If the dates and details of the Alpha celebration evening do not come up naturally in the discussion, this is a good time to mention them. Invitation cards can be handed out, too.

If possible, aim to pray together as a group at the end of this session.

### DISCUSSION

1. If you did not know anything about Christianity, how would you like to be told about it?

2. Has anyone told their friends / family / colleagues at work that they are doing Alpha? What was their reaction?

3. What do you think / feel about the idea of telling others?

## OPTIONAL BIBLE STUDY

**John 4:1–26**
**Jesus talks with a Samaritan woman**

1. What do we know about the woman?

2. How did Jesus initiate the conversation / contact? (v. 7)

3. How did Jesus present the gospel? Why did He present it like this to her? (vv. 10, 13, 14)

4. What does He mean by "living water" / "springs of water welling up to eternal life?"

5. Why does she start talking about "mountains?" (v. 20)

6. What does Jesus do about the red herring?

7. What does it mean to be "presented with Jesus?" (v. 26)

# DOES GOD HEAL TODAY?

## SESSION 12: DOES GOD HEAL TODAY?

### PRACTICAL

Remind people about the Alpha celebration evening. Try to work out approximately how many people will be coming, including small group members and any guests they plan to invite.

### DISCUSSION

If words of knowledge were given at the end of the talk, ask if anyone in the group thinks that a word of knowledge may have been appropriate for them.

If not, ask your guests if there is a specific problem or illness for which they would like prayer for healing. This is a good time to clear up any general issues about healing, so allow time for the group to discuss briefly before praying together.

Pray for people according to the ministry guidelines in this manual. If there are lots of people, divide into one group of men and one group of women.

Equally affirm those who do want to be prayed for and those who do not.

## SESSION 13: WHAT ABOUT THE CHURCH?

### PRACTICAL

Remind the group about the Alpha celebration evening. Try to finalize numbers.

Make a date for a small group reunion. This would possibly be at the host's house, ideally about two weeks before the next Alpha course starts.

### DISCUSSION

1. Go round the group, asking each person to summarize what they have learned and experienced over the past ten weeks. (Try to start and finish with an enthusiastic person!)

2. Ask the group what they would like to do after Alpha. Try to encourage them to stay connected as a group

3. Ask each of them if there is anything they would like prayer for

4. Pray—it's a good idea to finish the final evening with prayer

## OPTIONAL QUESTIONS FOR FURTHER DISCUSSION

1. What comes to mind when you hear the word "church" or "Christian?"

2. Look back on the last ten weeks. Has your view changed?

3. Looking forwards, in what way (if any) do you plan to continue what you've started on this Alpha course?

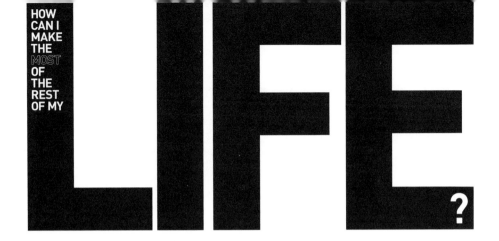

HOW
CAN I
MAKE
THE
MOST
OF
THE
REST
OF MY

LIFE?

## SESSION 14: HOW CAN I MAKE THE MOST OF THE REST OF MY LIFE?

### PRACTICAL

Spend time in your small group finding out how guests found the Alpha weekend. Allow guests to share their experiences and ask any questions. At the end, spend some time praying for any guests who wish to receive prayer.

# TEAM TRAININ

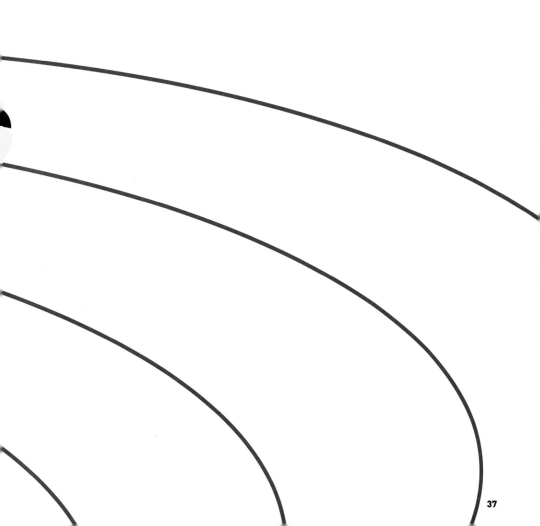

# HOS

# TING

SMALL GROUPS

## INTRODUCTION

The overall purpose of the small group, along with the course as a whole, is to help to bring people into a relationship with Jesus Christ.

Jesus Himself said that where two or three are gathered in His name, He is there also (Matthew 18:20).

- A group size of about twelve is ideal
- Jesus chose a group of twelve (Matthew 4:18–22)
- Each small group is made up of two hosts, two helpers, and approximately eight guests

**The six subsidiary aims of the small group:**

## 1. TO DISCUSS

The model for the Alpha small group is not teacher-pupil, but host-guest. Treat the people in your group as if they were guests in your own home—with honor, dignity, and respect.

Discuss the talk and issues arising from the message. It is vital to give people the opportunity to respond to what they have heard and to ask questions in a safe, nonthreatening environment.

### 1. Practical details
- Arrange the chairs so that guests can see and hear each other
- Ensure the host can see everyone
- Provide adequate lighting
- Check ventilation

- Keeping time—aim to start the discussion at 8:15 P.M. and end by 9:00 P.M.*

* Running times have been given as a guide only

### 2. Some groups are ruined by one of two things:

- Weak leadership—not properly prepared, allow one person do all the talking

- Dominant leadership—does all the talking, instead of giving people the freedom to speak and to say what is on their mind

### 3. Ask simple questions

- Two basic questions:

- What do you think?

- What do you feel?

- Avoid being patronizing. Guests may be new to Christianity, but they are not new to life. Treat everyone with respect and interest

- Direct questions back to the group: "What does everyone else think?"

### 4. Be prepared for questions

- Resource: *Searching Issues* by Nicky Gumbel, the seven issues most often raised on Alpha

# "PEOPLE ARE NEVER SO LIKELY AS TO SETTLE A QUESTION RIGHTLY AS WHEN THEY DISCUSS IT FREELY." THOMAS MACAULAY

## 2. TO MODEL BIBLE STUDY

With some groups, you may never get beyond discussion to Bible study. This applies especially to groups of nonchurchgoers or non-Christians.

If you do study the Bible as a group, the aim is to ask questions that get the guests looking at the passage and seeing things for themselves. If they see one thing for themselves from the passage, they will probably remember it for the rest of their lives. Only start a Bible study if everyone is ready. Always encourage others to talk, rather than giving a talk. Aim to motivate the group to start to read the Bible alone.

## 1. When you start

• Even if Bible study is planned, give everyone an opportunity to ask questions arising from hearing the talk or other questions on their minds

## 2. If the group is ready for Bible study, the host needs to prepare the passage carefully

(For suggested passages, see Section I of this manual—but be free to study any passage that you feel is appropriate)

• Read the passage beforehand (different versions): make sure you understand it

• Spot difficult verses: make sure you know answers from a commentary

## 3. Read passage

• Explain where it comes in the Bible

• Read either verse by verse, or ask one good reader to read the whole passage. Be sensitive to those who might not want to read

## 4. Give a short introduction

• In a sentence, give the main theme of the passage

• Explain at once any obviously difficult or ambiguous words (very little to be gained by asking "What does dissimulation mean?")

• Avoid (at all times) spiritual clichés, long words, and Christian jargon, which exclude the non-Christian and the new Christian

## 5. Get people talking

- Work out your questions carefully – short and simple (some examples are set out in Section I)
  - Not too hard
  - Not too easy – "Who died for us?"
  - Not too vague – "What is the difference between verses 7 and 17?"

- Ask open-ended questions, ("What?", "How?", "Who?" and "Why?") instead of closed questions (Yes/No answers)

- Aim to bring everyone into the discussion. Welcome everyone into the discussion. Encourage contribution from the quieter members of the group

- Basic questions:
  - "What does it say?"
  - "What does it mean?"
  - "How does it apply?"

- Learn as well as teach. Do not impose your own ideas

- Try not to answer your own questions yourself!

- Do not repeat someone's comment unless it needs alteration. If you cannot answer the question, do not bluff. Admit ignorance and either tackle the question afterwards or make a note and bring the answer next time. Better still; get someone else to do it!

## 6. Encouraging the group

- Smile and look interested
- Respond verbally to guests' comments:
  - "How interesting"
  - "I have never heard that before!"
  - "It might mean that . . ."

## 3. TO LEARN TO PRAY TOGETHER

Great sensitivity is required when praying together in the small group.

### 1. Opening prayer

- Either by you, or better still, by a member of the group
- To avoid embarrassment:
  - Put words into their mouth: "Will you ask God to give us wisdom to understand this passage . . .?"
  - If asking a member of the group, ask them beforehand (i.e., during dinner) so that it doesn't come as a surprise or put people off. Say to the group, "I have asked [X] to open in prayer"

### 2. End with prayer (if appropriate)

- Aim to start praying out loud together by session 7
- Long eloquent prayers may be impressive, but they discourage others from praying
- Model prayer e.g., "Father . . . (short sentence) . . . in Jesus' name, Amen."
- One of the hosts or helpers should hold themselves back from praying to remove pressure from any guests who may not want to pray

## 4. TO DEVELOP LASTING FRIENDSHIPS WITHIN THE BODY OF CHRIST

- The main reason why people stay in the church
- Get to know each person well
- Icebreaker games, e.g., name game (first night)
- Act as hosts
- Facilitates conversations
- Continue meeting together after the course is completed

## 5. TO LEARN TO MINISTER TO ONE ANOTHER

- Praying for each other
- Gifts of the Spirit

## 6. TO TRAIN OTHERS TO HOST

- People progress from guest to helper to host
- Delegation without training leads to disappointment (2 Timothy 2:2)

RÉ

## INTRODUCTION

# "THE BIBLE DOES NOTHING BUT SPEAK OF GOD'S LOVE." ST. AUGUSTINE

The Christian faith relies on our relationship with God and our relationships with others.

- God's love for us (Romans 5:5)
- Our relationship with God—the command to love God (Luke 10:27)
- Our relationship with others—the command to love one another (Mark 12:31)

The most important thing for a guest on Alpha is that they experience the love of God. This requires from us:

- Right motives
- Integrity of heart
- Love for others
- Skills to be learned

"We proclaim him, admonishing and teaching everyone with all wisdom, so that we may present everyone perfect in Christ. To this end I labor, struggling with all his energy, which so powerfully works in me." [Colossians 1:28-29]

## 1. AIM

### 1. Everyone

- Every single person on Alpha should be looked after
- Hosts divide up group to take pastoral responsibility for members
- The system must ensure every person is cared for
- Pray daily for each person

### 2. Spiritual maturity

- Not just Alpha—it's a lifelong process

- Follow up: home group
- Role in church
- Use of gifts

### 3. Maturity in Christ

- We do not want to attach people to ourselves
- Dependence should not be on us, but on Christ

## 2. METHOD

"We proclaim him, admonishing and teaching everyone with all wisdom . . ." (Colossians 1:28)

We grow in maturity as our intimacy with the Lord and our knowledge of Him grows.

### 1. Lead people to Jesus

- Resource: *Why Jesus?*

### 2. Encourage them to grow in their relationship with Jesus

- Bible study / prayer
- Christian books (see end of each chapter in *The Alpha Course Manual*)
- Listen to good Christian teaching

### 3. Encourage them to grow in their relationships within the body of Christ

- Alpha evenings
- Sundays
- Telephone/texts
- Reunions
- Continue meeting as a group

### 4. General attitude

- Be an encourager
- 1 Thessalonians 5:11
- Expressing warmth and responsiveness
- Be positive

- Be a listener (not always a teacher)
- James 1:19–26
- Draw people out
- Listening models respect and gives people their dignity
- Be a peacemaker
- Matthew 5:9
- Reconciling differences, relieving tension, and exploring reasons for differences (diplomatically)

## 3. COMMITMENT

"To this end I labor, struggling with all his energy, which so powerfully works in me." (Colossians 1:29)

### 1. Our responsibility

- "I labor, struggling"
- Commitment to pray

- Hard work
- Effort
- Late nights
- Overcoming tiredness
- Not talking to old friends, but welcoming new people
- Efficiency with jobs
- Overcoming disappointment

### 2. God's grace

- ". . . with all his energy . . ." (Colossians 1:29)
- Be filled with the Spirit—"full of faith and of the Holy Spirit" (Acts 6:5)
- Try to allow the Spirit of God to speak to you during the talks and fill you during worship/ministry

But

- Then be ready to serve

- Use every gift:
- Evangelism
- Teaching
- Pastoring
- Prophetic—hearing God

# PRAYE
# MINIS

ON ALPHA

## INTRODUCTION

The activity of the Holy Spirit transforms every aspect of the Alpha course.

- The word "ministry" is used in several different senses in the New Testament
- Broadly, "ministry" means "service" —includes everything done on Alpha
- Ministry is, "Meeting the needs of others on the basis of God's resources" (John Wimber)
- "Ministry" referring to "prayer ministry"—"come Holy Spirit"
- Cooperation between God and us (Exodus 14:16, 21–22)
- Opportunities for prayer ministry during the course
- Alpha weekend (Saturday evening and Sunday morning)
- Healing evening

## 1. THE MINISTRY OF THE HOLY SPIRIT – FIVE VALUES

### 1. When we ask the Holy Spirit to come, He comes

- Get our perspective right (Luke 10:17–20)
- The branch must look principally at the vine and not at the fruit

### 2. Because it is His ministry, we aim for simplicity and truthfulness in all aspects of our prayers for people

- Avoid intensity (shouting, religious language, eccentricity)
- Be yourself (be normal, natural, pray in your normal voice)

### 3. Face the person you are praying for and ask the Holy Spirit to come

- Welcome Him when you see signs of His working and wait on God for further directions

- Don't worry about silence

**4. Silently ask God what He wants to do or to say . . . how to encourage and how to impart gifts**

- Prophecy is always strengthening, encouraging, comforting (1 Corinthians 14:3)

**5. Ask what is happening**

- "What do you sense is happening?"

- "Do you sense God saying something?"

## 2. BIBLICAL AUTHORITY

**1. The Spirit of God and the written Word of God never conflict**

- The truth sets us free (John 8:32)

- Paul's prayer—Ephesians 3:17-19

**2. Build on biblical truths and promises, e.g.:**

- Guilt (Romans 8:1)
- Repentance (Psalm 51)
- Fear (Psalm 91)
- Guidance (Psalm 37:5)
- Temptation (1 Corinthians 10:13)
- Anxiety (Philippians 4:6–7)

**3. Say how you are going to pray and encourage faith in a particular promise of God**

- Hold on to God's promises. One aspect of faith is the finding of a promise of God and daring to believe it!

## 3. THE DIGNITY OF THE INDIVIDUAL

- Confidentiality is essential
- Pray for people in relaxed surroundings (either on your own or in pairs)
- Men pray with men, women pray with women
- Respect privacy
- Affirm—do not condemn
- Faith—do not place additional burdens on people
- Allow them freedom to come back!
- Take time to sort out difficulties of understanding, belief, and assurance
- Lead to Christ (resource: *Why Jesus?*)
- Fullness of the Spirit
- "Am I ready?"
- "I am unworthy"
- "I could never speak in another language"

  1 Corinthians 14:2, 4,14; Matthew 7:11

- If a guest wants to receive, encourage the person to start to speak in another language—tell him/her you will do so also

## 4. HARMONIOUS RELATIONSHIPS

"May they be brought to complete unity to let the world know that you sent me and have loved them even as you have loved me." (John 17:23)

### 1. Unity comes from the Holy Spirit

- Lack of unity, love, and forgiveness hinders the work of the Spirit
- One person should take a lead in praying for others rather than compete with conflicting prayers

## 5. THE BODY OF CHRIST

**1. The Christian community is the place where long-term healing and spiritual growth take place under the protective umbrella of the authority of a church**

- Allow people to move at their own pace, remembering that it is a process

**2. Keep in touch**

- Warn against possible increased temptation

- Refuse to consider that "nothing has happened"

- Ephesians 5:18—go on being filled with the Spirit

# HAS THE ALPHA COURSE CHANGED YOUR LIFE?

### Did you know?
Thousands of people just like you have recently completed the Alpha course. Stay connected to hear news and stories, as well as how you can get involved in touching other people's lives. Become a prayer partner or volunteer because at Alpha we are always looking for people to use their skills to help others learn about Jesus.

### Tell us your story
Has your life been changed on an Alpha course? We would love to hear how God worked in your life. It might be just what someone considering attending an Alpha course needs to hear to take the step to attend. www.alphausa.org/mystory   www.alphacanada.org/stories

### Bible program
Bible in One Year with Nicky and Pippa Gumbel – Sign up today for a daily email devotional that coordinates with the Bible in One Year reading plan.

www.alphausa.org/bibleinoneyear
www.alphacanada.org/bibleinoneyear
www.alpha.org/bioy (Caribbean and Latin America)

### Join our online communities
Join the conversation with people across the country who have participated in Alpha as guests and volunteers.

Facebook.com - Alpha USA; Alpha Canada; Alpha Caribbean; Alpha Latin America

Twitter - www.twitter.com/alphausa; @alphalatam; @alphacanada

Not all of these programs are available in all countries. Please visit www.alpha.org.